MICHAEL HEATH'S
The BAttle FOR BRItain

WP

WP

Published by:
Wilkinson Publishing Pty Ltd
ACN 006 042 173
Level 4, 2 Collins St Melbourne, Victoria, Australia 3000
Ph: +61 3 9654 5446
www.wilkinsonpublishing.com.au

Every effort has been made to ensure that this book is free
from error or omissions. However, the Publisher, the Authors,
the Editor or their respective employees or agents, shall not
accept responsibility for injury, loss or damage occasioned
to any person acting or refraining from action as a result
of material in this book whether or not such injury, loss or
damage is in any way due to any negligent act or omission,
breach of duty or default on the part of the Publisher, the
Authors, the Editor, or their respective employees or agents.

National Library of Australia Cataloguing-in-Publication entry:
Creator: Heath, Michael, author.
Title: Michael Heath's the battle for Britain / Michael Heath.
ISBN: 9781925642087 (paperback).
Subjects: Political cartoons.
           English wit and humor, Pictorial.
           Caricatures and cartoons--Great Britain.
           Great Britain--Politics and government--
           Caricatures and cartoons.

Printed in Australia
Design: Michael Bannenberg

I don't want you to think I am a whiny old lefty – I am not! I am neither left·nor right, I just observe what I see around me. I'd be lost without humourless teens on their mobiles or indeed everyone on their mobiles, staring at them in the vain hope that something or someone will make them famous! It's the addiction to the mobile phone that makes me feel out of it.

I decided to have a go at the reality that I saw around me. Cartoons, to be of any use, should always be about reality. Hopefully this little book will cheer you up! Thank you Australia for putting all the cartoons together in one book. With a bit of luck I will join you one day to say G'day!

HEATH

Michael Heath M.B.E
Cartoon editor of The Spectator *magazine*

For Gareth, Seral and David at the *Spectator*
and of course the editor Fraser Nelson.
And Hilary, Clare and Charlie on the home front.

2013

these are the EARLY STRIPS
I DID FOR THE BATTLE FOR BRITAIN

LATER I FOUND I WAS GOING TO
GET MORE MATERIAL OBSERVING
WHAT I SAW AROUND ME.

MAY 4, 2013

This is the prequel, if you like, to the BFB.

AUGUST 3, 2013

AUGUST 10, 2013

AUGUST 31, 2013

SEPTEMBER 7, 2013

SEPTEMBER 14, 2013

SEPTEMBER 28, 2013

9

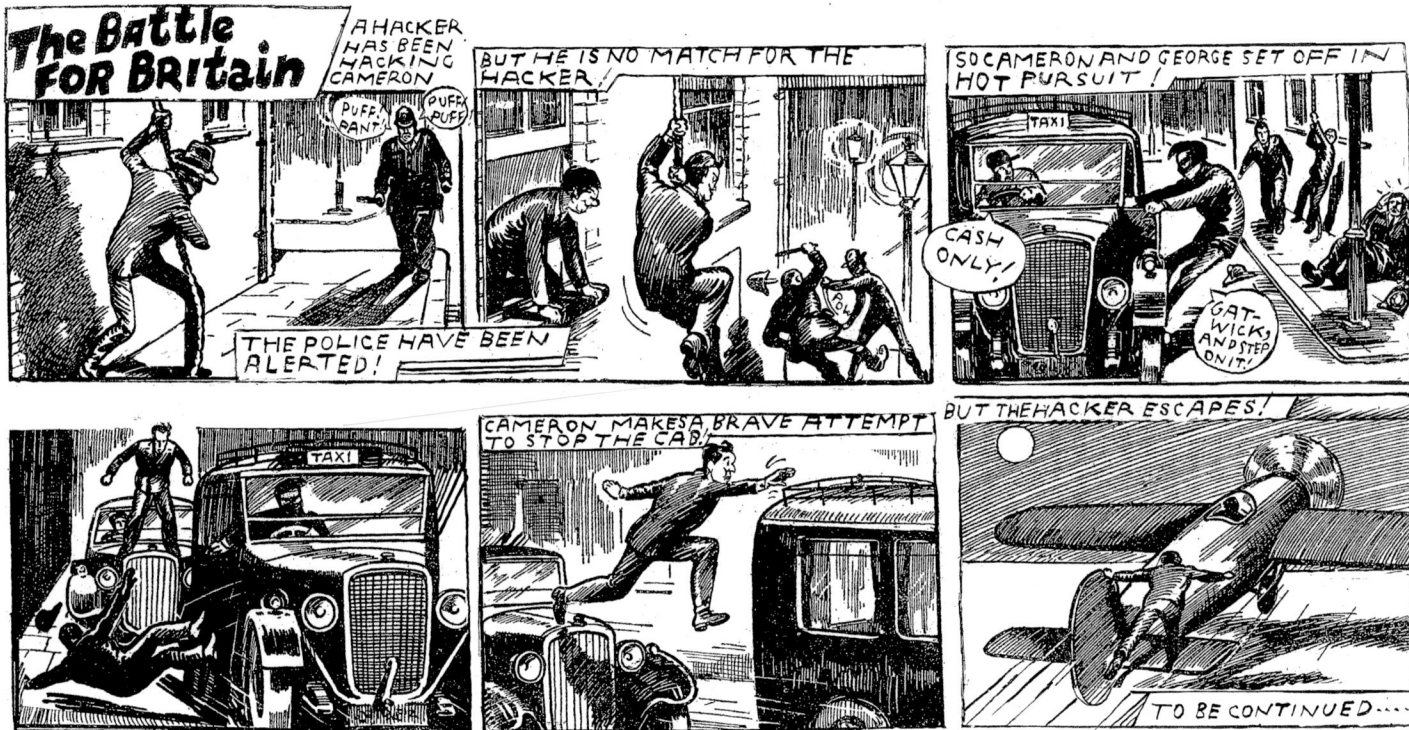

OCTOBER 5, 2013

OCTOBER 12, 2013

OCTOBER 19, 2013

OCTOBER 26, 2013

DECEMBER 7, 2013

The real BFB starts here!

DECEMBER 14, 2013

2014

IF POLITICAL CORRECTNESS DRIVES YOU CRAZY AND GENDERBENDING AND MOBILE PHONE ADDICTIONS WORRY YOU, THEN THEN THIS IS THE COLLECTION FOR YOU!

JANUARY 1, 2014

JANUARY 18, 2014

JANUARY 25, 2014

21

The Battle FOR Britain

JACK HAD WRITTEN A SCRIPT FOR A MOVIE CALLED 'INANE' AND HOLLYWOOD CALLED, OFFERING HIM $20M FOR IT! I WAS SO JEALOUS I DECIDED TO KIDNAP AND KILL HIM!

I TOOK HIM TO A TO A DESERTED PLACE, WHERE NO ONE WENT ANY MORE.'

FEBRUARY 1, 2014

FEBRUARY 8, 2014

23

FEBRUARY 15, 2014

FEBRUARY 22, 2014

MARCH 1, 2014

MARCH 8, 2014

The Battle FOR Britain

SAMANTHA WAS CRYING BECAUSE SHE WAS SO LONELY

HER SO CALLED FRIENDS, WOULDN'T TALK TO HER!

WHEN SHE EXPLAINED THIS TO HER MOTHER'S NEW PARTNER ALEX, SHE TOLD SAMANTHA THAT SHE KNEW JUST THE ANSWER!

MARCH 29, 2014

APRIL 5, 2014

29

APRIL 12, 2014

APRIL 19, 2014

Relationships, marriage... men losing the plot...

APRIL 26, 2014

BLAND showbiz interviews...

MAY 17, 2014

33

MAY 24, 2014

JUNE 14, 2014

The Battle FOR Britain

PARENTS!

ARE YOU AWARE WHAT YOUR TEENAGE CHILDREN GET UP TO AT WEEKENDS? THIS IS A TYPICAL SCENE OF AN ALL NIGHT RAVE IN SHOREDITCH, LONDON! HOT CHOCOLATE DRINKS, BUNS, AND LEMONADE ARE CONSUMED QUITE OPENLY! AND THE POLICE TURN A BLIND EYE!

JUNE 21, 2014

JULY 5, 2014

JULY 26, 2014

AUGUST 2, 2014

Does anyone remember loom bands?

SANDY HAD BEEN SENT A LETTER HAND WRITTEN, IN INK ON PAPER. SHE'D NEVER SEEN A HAND WRITTEN LETTER BEFORE, ONLY E-MAILS!

IT WAS FROM HER BOY-FRIEND. HE BEGGED TO SEE HER.

MR ROMANCE!

WE CAN'T AFFORD TO BUY A HOUSE! SO I THINK WE SHOULD START A TREND— CAVE DWELLING! WE WILL BE CAVE DWELLERS!

AUGUST 9, 2014

AUGUST 16, 2014

Girls' relationships with their mothers.

AUGUST 23, 2014

AUGUST 30, 2014

THIS WEEK I'M TALKING TO CLAIR SEAWEED, DESIGNER OF LIFE. 'I HAVEN'T EATEN FOR SIX MONTHS, MY LIFE DEMANDS THAT! SHE LAUGHS AND SHRIEKS AT THE SAME! THE ONLY WAY SHE KNOWS HOW TO RELAX IS PERFORMING BRAIN SURGERY. THE RESULTS MAY NOT ALWAYS BE SATISFACTORY, BUT AS SHE SAYS 'IT HELPS KEEP ME GROUNDED'.

MONDAY IS THE NEW TUESDAY

TOOTH-PASTE IS SO OVER

NOTTING HILL GATE IS NOW IN LOCKDOWN WAITING FOR HER NEW WINTER LINGERIE COLLECTION- PANTIES HONED FROM CORK, BRAS HAMMERED FROM SPITTOONS ...

CLAIR SEAWEED DESIGNER OF LIFESTYES, CLOTHES FACILITATOR, BRAIN SURGEON, AND LAST BUT NOT LEAST—MOTHER!

SEPTEMBER 6, 2014

SEPTEMBER 13, 2014

45

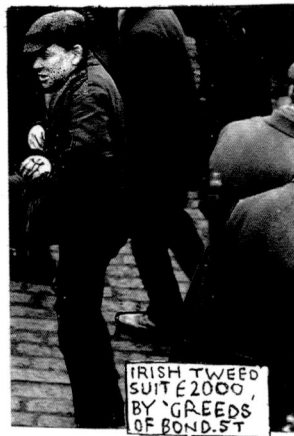

SEPTEMBER 20, 2014

Are you ready for The New Austerity 2?

The Battle FOR Britain

SADLY, JUSTINE AND VIOLET WERE FINDING OUT
THAT THERE WERE CERTAIN PARTS OF
LONDON WHERE ONE DIDN'T GO AROUND
SHOWING OFF YOUR LATEST E-PHONE!

SEPTEMBER 27, 2014

OCTOBER 4, 2014

Some people have appalling points of view.

OCTOBER 11, 2014

Theatre will never die.

The Battle For Britain

BEING FORCED TO HAVE SEX WITH HER HUSBAND MADE LOUISE SO DISTRAUGHT THAT SHE STARTED UP A REVENGE PORN SITE.

OCTOBER 18, 2014

You never really know people, do you?

OCTOBER 25, 2014

Some men never learn.

THIS IMMIGRATION BUSINESS IS GETTING OUT OF CONTROL!

NOVEMBER 6, 2014

NOVEMBER 8, 2014

P.C. panic! The over 35-year-old male has lost the plot.

NOVEMBER 15, 2014

Expensive bag hell!

NOVEMBER 22, 2014

Men not sure how to behave.

55

2015

WHEN RELATIONSHIPS OF EVERY COMBINATION
AND "O.M.G" AND WHITE T-SHIRTS AND TATTOOING
WERE DE RIGUEUR...

The Battle for Britain

LOOK, MUMMY I THINK WE SHOULD TALK. YOU SEE I'VE MET ANOTHER MOTHER AND SHE UNDERSTANDS ME AND SHE'S FUN. SO I'M GOING TO LIVE WITH HER FROM NOW ON.

JANUARY 3, 2015

Families are being rent asunder.

ILLEGAL SEX THERAPISTS ARE FLOODING THE COUNTRY... NOW READ ON...

THE SEX THERAPIST'S DAUGHTERS SET OUT TO SEND ALL THE FOREIGN SEX THERAPISTS PACKING!

JANUARY 17, 2015

The Battle FOR BRITAIN

JANUARY 24, 2015

Blitz 1 - 1940, Blitz 2 - 2015

THE GIRLS WERE ALWAYS EMBARRASSED BY THEIR MOTHER

JANUARY 31, 2015

The eternal conflict.

FEBRUARY 7, 2015

Or does it?

FEBRUARY 14, 2015

Life is complicated nowadays.

FEBRUARY 21, 2015

The Battle FOR Britain

24 7 BURGERS

THE GIRLS SOON REALISED THAT CERTAIN POST CODES IN LONDON HAD NOT YET BEEN GENTRIFIED!

FEBRUARY 28, 2015

Location, location, location.

MARCH 21, 2015

White t-shirt rage.

APRIL 4, 2015

Hair today, gone tomorrow.

The Battle For Britain

AT LAST, HE HAD REALISED HIS DREAM. A SITE WITH PLANNING PERMISSION FOR FOURTY HOMES AND A SHOPPING MALL

REEDS ESTATE AGENT LAND FOR SALE

APRIL 11, 2015

Someone is always on the lookout to make a quick buck.

NEXT SUMMER THEY WOULD GO ABROAD, AS THE WEATHER IN ENGLAND WAS SO UNPREDICTABLE!

APRIL 25, 2015

The Battle for Britain

GIRLS IN THE MOBILE PHONE ADDICTION CLINIC LEARN HOW TO SURVIVE FOR ONE HOUR WITHOUT A PHONE!

MAY 2, 2015

MAY 23, 2015

MAY 30, 2015

The Battle for Britain

OFFICER! OFFICER! GHASTLY RICH HEDGEFUNDERS ETC ARE DESTROYING THIS ONCE CHARMING AREA BY DIGGING DOWN INTO THE BASEMENTS OF THEIR BEAUTIFUL EDWARDIAN HOUSES AND CONSTRUCTING AWFUL GYMS, WITH SWIMMING POOLS AND ENTERTAINMENT COMPLEXES!...

JUNE 6, 2015

Too true.

JUNE 13, 2015

JUNE 20, 2015

1939

2015

CAN YOU SPOT THE 10 DIFFERENCES BETWEEN THESE TWO PICTURES OF FAMILY LIFE?

JUNE 27, 2015

Fings ain't what they used to be.

JULY 4, 2015

The Battle for Britain

SINCE APPEARING ON 'STRICTLY' PATSY HAD ACQUIRED QUITE A FAN BASE IN THE VILLAGE!

JULY 18, 2015

JULY 25, 2015

AUGUST 8, 2015

Children on tap.

AUGUST 15, 2015

Equality at last!

The Battle For Britain

THE WEEK END RESIDENTS OF THE VILLAGE WERE HUGELY JEALOUS OF THE YOKEL FOR BEING ABLE TO GET SUPER FAST RECEPTION BY ERECTING HIS OWN BROAD BAND RECEIVER

AUGUST 22, 2015

83

SEPTEMBER 5, 2015

SEPTEMBER 12, 2015

Less is more.

SEPTEMBER 19, 2015

87

OCTOBER 10, 2015

To thine own self be true.

OCTOBER 24, 2015

The Battle FOR BRITAIN

OCTOBER 31, 2015

Some people are so selfie.

The Battle for Britain

THERE'S NO DOUBT ABOUT IT, THOUGHT RONALD, AS HE VIEWED OXFORD ST FROM HIS HOTEL. I'VE BEEN AWAY FROM LONDON TOO LONG. IT'S CHANGED!

NOVEMBER 7, 2015

The Battle FOR Britain

ALTERNATIVE COMEDIAN

ROGER'S CAREER AS A STAND-UP COMIC IS IN FREEFALL, AND HE HAS NO IDEA WHY.

O.M.G.!- THAT'S SO NOT FUNNY!

CAN'T LIVE WITH THEM, CAN'T LIVE WITHOUT THEM! NOW TAKE MY GENDER FLUID WIFE! PLEASE!. (SINGS) CROSS DRESSERS DO GET WEARY, WEARING THE SAME SHABBY DRESS..

GASP!

NOVEMBER 14, 2015

2016

COSMETIC SURGERY AND BOTOX TAKE OFF, WITH IMMIGRATION, AND BEING GENDERFLUID....

The Battle FOR Britain

WHAT THE BOYS LOVED THE MOST WAS BEING READ EXCERPTS FROM NIGELLA'S LATEST COOKBOOK AROUND THE CAMP FIRE

JANUARY 2, 2016

Boys will be boys.

NOBODY, BUT NOBODY, COULD GET GLENDA TO WEAR A SEAT BELT!

JANUARY 16, 2016

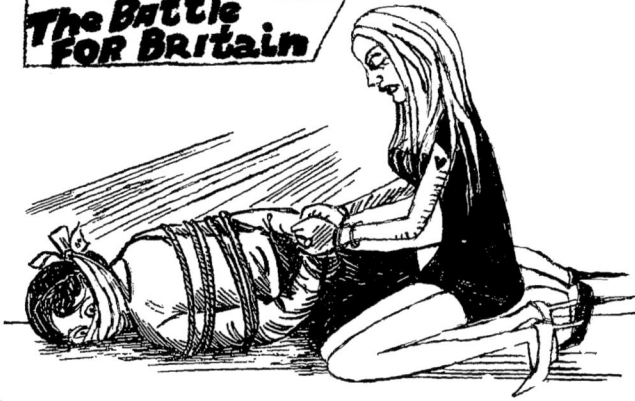

JANUARY 23, 2016

FEBRUARY 6, 2016

FEBRUARY 20, 2016

FEBRUARY 27, 2016

MARCH 5, 2016

MARCH 12, 2016

Some women are never happy.

The Battle for Britain

THE DAY THAT ALL PHONE SIGNALS DIED!

MARCH 19, 2016

103

The Battle for Britain

WITH A MASSIVE LOAN, THEY WERE ABLE TO PUT DOWN A DEPOSIT ON THEIR NEW HOME

MARCH 26, 2016

The Battle for Britain

WELL, I THINK THEIR REWORKING OF NOEL'S 'PRIVATE LIVES' FOR A CONTEMPORARY AUDIENCE REALLY WORKS!

APRIL 2, 2016

This one will run and run.

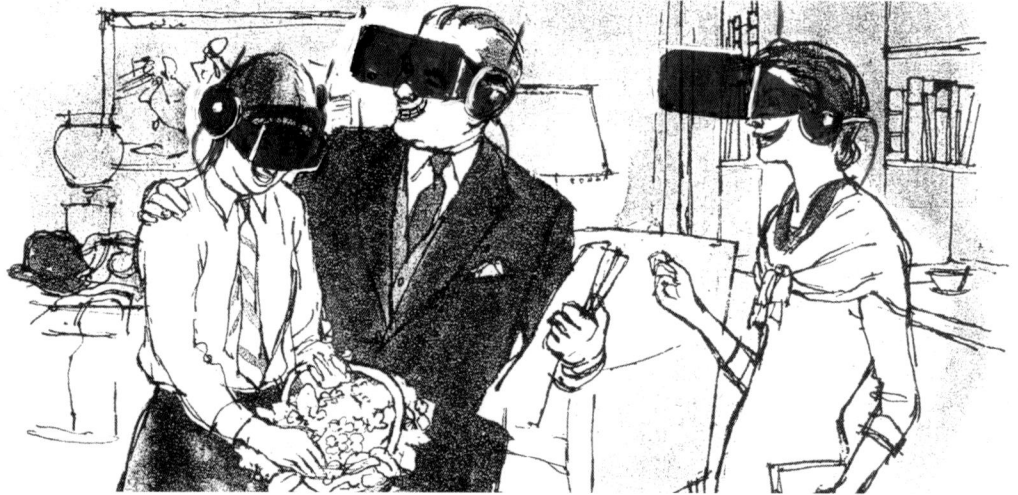

The Battle For Britain

NOW THAT HER DAD HAD BOUGHT THEM ALL VIRTUAL REALITY GADGETS, JENNY FELT THEY WERE A HAPPY UNITED FAMILY AGAIN!

APRIL 9, 2016

APRIL 16, 2016

Top Gear!

The Battle FOR Britain

BECAUSE SHE DIDN'T SHARE HER HUSAND'S OBSESSION WITH PORNOGRAPHY ONLINE, THE EVENINGS WERE OFTEN SPENT IN TOTAL SILENCE

APRIL 23, 2016

SHE WAS SOON TO FIND OUT THE COOLEST RESTAURANT HAD THE WORST SERVICE

MAY 14, 2016

Food for thought.

MAY 21, 2016

The Battle FOR Britain

MAYBE THE DOCTOR HAD BEEN RIGHT. THE PILLS SEEM TO BE HAVING THE DESIRED EFFECT! HE NO LONGER WANTED TO WATCH 'TOP GEAR' OR 'STRICTLY' EVER AGAIN!

MAY 28, 2016

YOU HAVE NO IDEA WHAT IT'S LIKE COMING OUT AS STRAIGHT. IN A MILLION YEARS I COULDN'T HAVE IMAGINED WHAT I WAS IN FOR! THE WORRY ABOUT LOSING MY HAIR, PUTTING ON WEIGHT, WATCHING 'BRITAINS GOT TALENT' WITH A WIFE WHO'S PUT YOU ON NO-SPEAKS, SPENDING £750 TO SEE 'LION KING' AND STAYING IN SOME GOD AWFUL HOTEL.....

The Battle FOR Britain

JUNE 4, 2016

Straight pride.

The Battle FOR Britain

WHAT PEOPLE DON'T SEEM TO UNDERSTAND, THAT ONCE OUT OF THE LIMELIGHT, HAIRDRESSERS LEAD ONE HELLUVA TOUGH LIFE!

JUNE 11, 2016

THE THOUGHT
OF AGEING SO
TERRIFIED
RONNIE THAT
HE STARTED
USING BOTOX

JUNE 25, 2016

The Battle for Britain

COMING TO TV SOON! A SEARING NEW VERSION OF REBECCA OF SUNNYBROOK FARM!

JULY 2, 2016

Updating a classic.

FREEDOM OF SPEECH

JULY 9, 2016

JULY 16, 2016

The Battle FOR Britain

EVERY YEAR
THEY LOOKED FORWARD
TO THE FESTIVAL
OF THE PHONES –
AND EVERY YEAR
IT BECAME MORE
ENCHANTING!

JULY 30, 2016

A cause for celebration.

The Battle for Britain

ST BARTS

SPORTS DAY

LASHINGS OF GINGER BEER AND JAM SANDWICHES ARE NOT CLASSIFIED AS ENERGY ENHANCING DRUGS, SO GLENDA WON EVERY RACE ON ST BARTS SCHOOL FOR GIRLS SPORTS DAY!

LONG JUMP

AUGUST 6, 2016

AUGUST 13, 2016

AUGUST 20, 2016

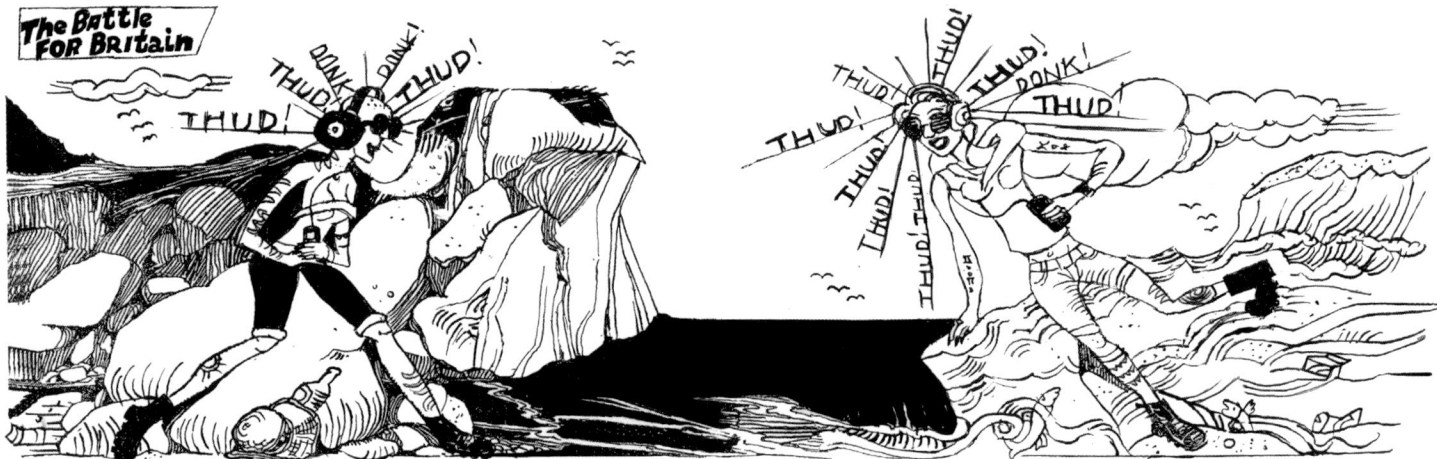

THE GIRLS LOVED TO GET OUT OF LONDON, AND COMMUNE WITH NATURE

AUGUST 27, 2016

SEPTEMBER 3, 2016

Phone Fido!

THE SIDE EFFECTS OF THE PARTY PILL SHE HAD TAKEN WERE RATHER ODD!

SEPTEMBER 17, 2016

Changing times.

SEPTEMBER 24, 2016

125

OCTOBER 1, 2016

Happy memories without a mobile phone.

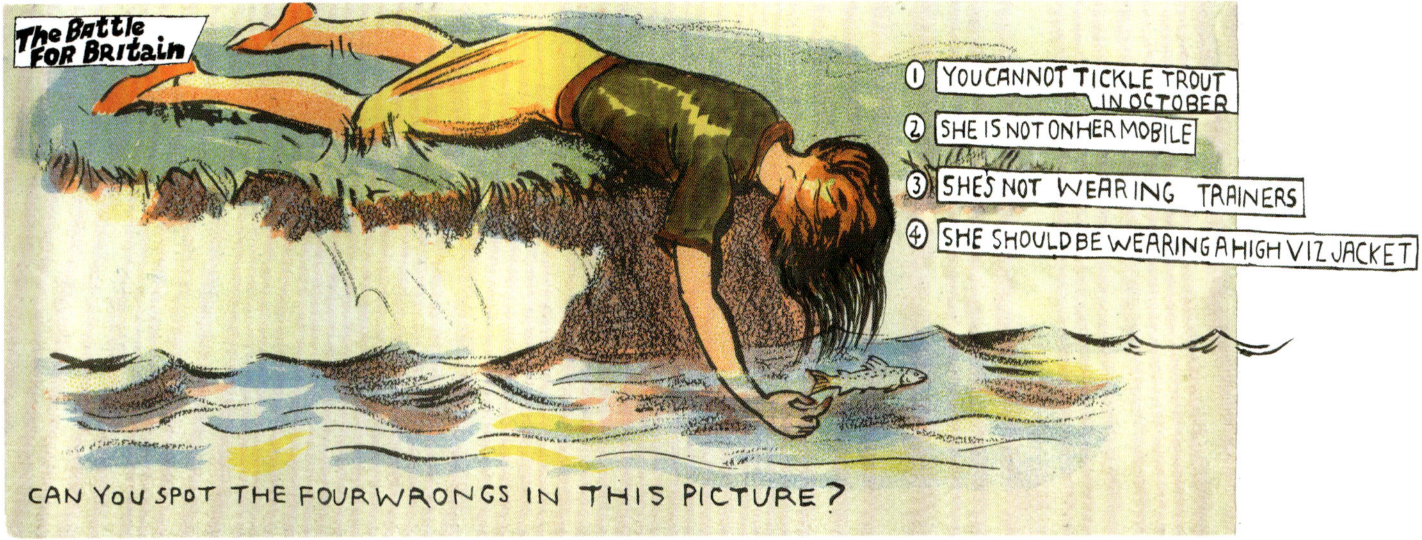

OCTOBER 8, 2016

OCTOBER 15, 2016

Rescue dog.

The Battle for Britain

WOW! WHAT A DAY!
MY FIRST VAMPIRE
FACE LIFT! AND
SOME MICRO-
NEEDLING ON
MY LIPS!
I ALSO ORDERED
A BOTTOM LIFT
FOR THE NEW
YEAR, AND HAD MY
FACE THREADED...

OCTOBER 22, 2016

Beauty treatment.

129

ARRIVALS

The Battle FOR BRITAIN

IT IS ASSUMED THAT EVERYONE WHO TURNS UP AT OUR BORDERS IS ALLOWED TO STAY

OCTOBER 29, 2016

THE BATTLE FOR BRITAIN

THESE SHOCKING PICTURES HAVE COME TO LIGHT OF LIFE BEFORE THE MOBILE PHONE.

NOVEMBER 5, 2016

Reading lesson.

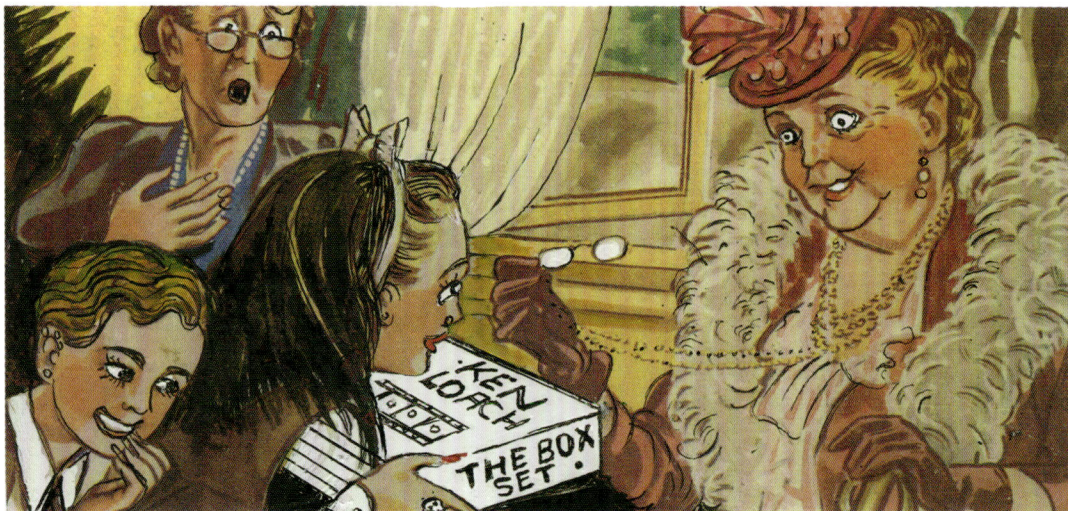

NOVEMBER 19, 2016

NOVEMBER 26, 2016

Stage fright.

DECEMBER 3, 2016

2017

HARD BREXIT COMES ALONG WITH `LOVE ISLAND'
THE BATTLE FOR BRITAIN
STILL GOES ON....

JANUARY 7, 2017

Bag for life.

JANUARY 28, 2017

Cruelty to children.

FEBRUARY 4, 2017

Stressed out.

FEBRUARY 11, 2017

The Battle FOR Britain

AN EXCLUSIVE PREVIEW OF ONE
BALLET DANCER'S RAGE AGAINST
BREXIT

FEBRUARY 18, 2017

FEBRUARY 25, 2017

All at sea.

MARCH 4, 2017

Split ends.

MARCH 11, 2017

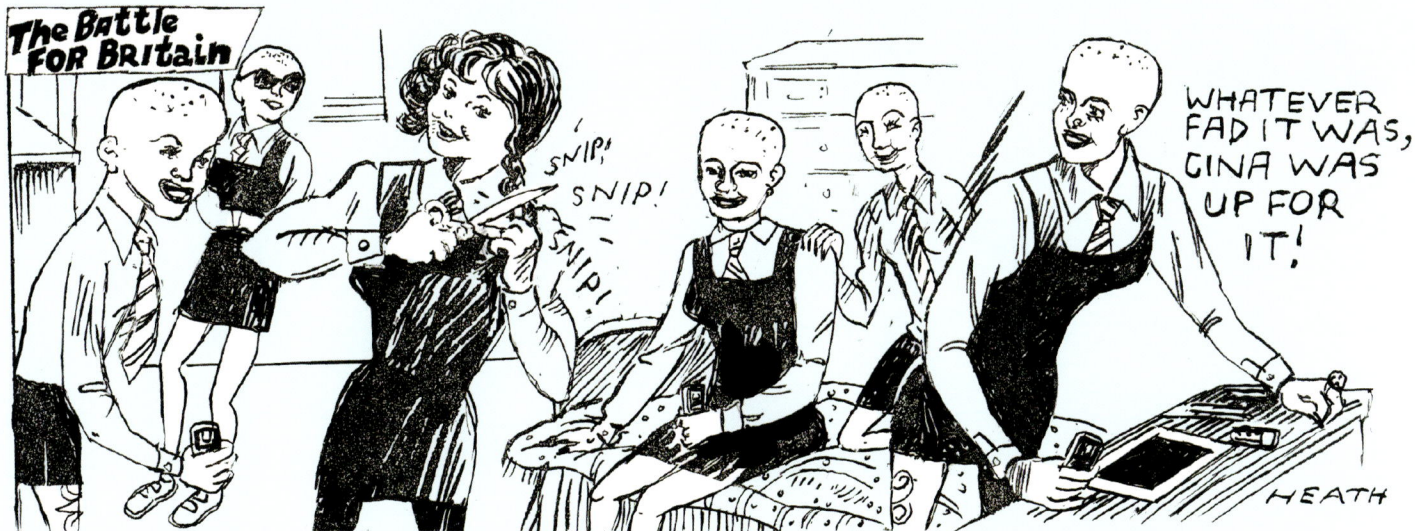

MARCH 18, 2017

Passing fads.

The Battle for Britain

PLAY FOR TODAY... A YOUNG MIXED RACE GIRL IS DRIVEN TO SELF-HARMING BY HER BREXIT PARENTS. SHE RUNS AWAY TO LIVE WITH SOME CROSS DRESSERS LIVING IN A BUS SHELTER... A CASTING DIRECTOR FROM 'BAKE OFF' DISCOVERS HER...

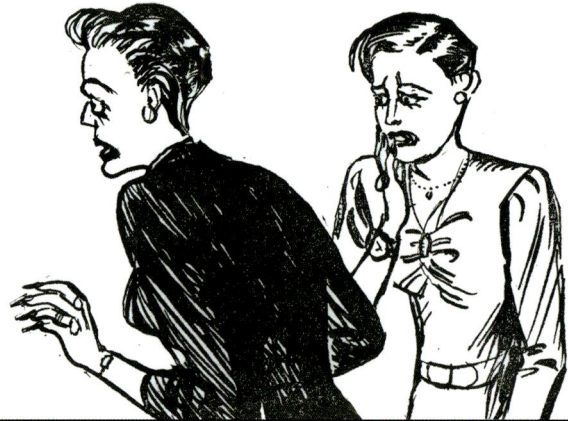

MARCH 25, 2017

Radio drama.

JULY 29, 2017

TV drama.

MICHAEL HEATH
INTERVIEW

8 April 2017 with Hillary Penn

H: Hello Michael, we're here to talk about you. Can you tell us a story about your childhood, the war, you running around?

M: OK – you must understand I am sick of being interviewed and talking about myself. The Police are now coming to get me.

H: Yeah yeah!

M: My first memories are about the beginning of the war, I was born in 1935, and I was not evacuated but my parents thought it would be best if I stayed with one of my grandmothers in Devon. I think my mother came too. The war had just started and it was assumed it would be over in a year or less and I would return to London. I wasn't long in Devon and I was sitting on a beach, which wasn't easy to do as it was scaffolded to protect you from mines. It was a lovely warm day, I got down on the beach and sat there, I remember two soldiers in front of me. The men separated and two aircraft came over. Where we were was in a bay near Plymouth, which at that time was being bombed badly. The soldiers said, oh look they're one of ours. Anyway the planes separated and cannon fired us along the beach. I got up and just started running. The idea was I shouldn't have run. They dropped a bomb on the village not far away. I got up on the promenade and there was clatter clatter clatter all around me. It was caused by red hot shrapnel falling from the bomb. All around me were various people lying in the road who'd been blown up and were dead. After that I managed to get home and I don't remember that much about it. It was considered at the time that it was probably more dangerous in the country than in London so soon after that I came back to London.

You'd better ask me about my father and all that hadn't you?

My father, like all other fathers at that period, was distant from me. All parents were, it seemed to me then. They didn't get close up and cuddle you and all that. You were made to look after yourselves, thrown out in the morning and come back at dinner time.

He was working as an ARP – Air Raid Patrol – he had a blue uniform with a badge. He was responsible for looking after the people of half of Hampstead, if they were bombed or houses were on fire or displaced. Also keeping an eye on us, London was under the blitz. To me as a child it didn't seem frightening. My parents never went in the underground or in an air raid shelter. I thought it was vaguely exciting, God knows why. I made friends and we had a little gang that we would run around in. The main problem was old men, we called them Beefers. There were funny old pedophiles at the time going around offering you toffee, also with the ability to take us into the cinema to see a H (horror) movie or an adult movie and fiddle with us. I always made my excuses and left but that was the main feature I remember about it. Also collecting incendiary bombs that were dropped too low. They were littered over Hampstead Heath and my father asked me go round with a few friends and pick up. We then took them to the Freemason's Arms where we piled them up like milk bottles in the garage. They were very tricky things that could explode at any moment but I had seen what my father did with them and followed that. In fact it was part of the adventure of being involved in this conflict at the age of six or seven. At the time there was very little school because when there was an air raid you were told to go to the basement and stay there. I used to break away and run back down the hill again. I was convinced my house was being bombed, which it wasn't.

My father, not only was he a warden, but he also illustrated children's comics. He wasn't trying to be funny like I do. He did gangster strips and cowboys strips, he was very good at horses, which I am not I have just found out. (Grand National cartoon in the *Mail* on Sunday 9th April 2017).

I got on well enough with my mother who now I realise had a great influence on me that at the time I did not realise. It's amazing I didn't turn into a ballet dancer. She informed me about all sorts of things that I don't think young boys should have been told, such as what the Gestapo would do to their enemies, about torture. She would take me out and lose me, like to the

cinema, or hair dressers where they would clip round the edges with a bowl on your head. In this case she took me to the hairdressers and I had to sit on a plank over the chair and tied to it as I hated it. She would hide from me where ever she could, I can only assume my mother was having affairs with various military men in the village. I couldn't prove this and wouldn't say it in court! But I think something was going on. This left me with a feeling on anxiety about being left. I have been tortured by this all my life. Anyway the war carried on and Hampstead was a very arty place a bit like Soho was a few years ago. I got to know people up there a bit by looking at them. Many of them were refugees from Nazi Germany, Polish – all Jewish. The atmosphere I grew up in was one of intellectuality. My father was a socialist, for the workers who thought Joe Stalin was the answer to life. As they used to say "All them cornfields and ballet in the evening". And his friends were also communists, it was considered a rather elite thing to do. They thought Churchill was a war monger. My father read a daily newspaper, I say this as hardly anyone does anymore, the kids don't. *The Daily Mirror* was a socialist newspaper then, Hugh Cudlip and various other writers. I picked that up now and then. On the wall at home there were various woodcuts, Van Gogh and others, obviously not real ones, prints and all sorts of things that other kids wouldn't see. Intelligent books, Left wing book club, God help us. Nobody could read them but still. Orange unreadable things. I was brought up by free, easy going parents who didn't force me to try to read or go back to school or anything like that. There were no cars or dinner parties, no theatre. Amongst this my father was doing all these drawings of cowboys and Indians and I gather hated it but I didn't go into it too deeply. But he hated it.

Within this a man turns up who was a friend of my parents before the war and he's really rich, he's running a shop selling old maps, opposite Claridges, Mayfair or whatever. He was very sophisticated in that he had his cigarettes with his initials on them, he'd buy these in Burlington Arcade. He chain smoked, they were huge things with no tips or anything like that. His hands were brown, his moustache was brown. Anyway he was full of stories, he'd been everywhere, done everything.

I thought he was particularly intriguing. I think he was an old boyfriend of my mother. My father would disappear whenever he arrived. He had jewellery and a lighter that had been made in Russia, all this expensive largess around him. Expensive clothing. He'd go away and you'd see him in six months. So I saw that side of life. He went to America for five minutes and hated it. He went to New York and brought me some expensive toys that you couldn't get in England like Mickey Mouse on a railway line and various other things. I think I had a teddy. Some how this was wrong as it was removed from me in 24 hours and given to the kids next door. I didn't have toys or books except for the odd old annual. Again there was this funny atmosphere and once in a while a relative would turn up, a man who was working in London to go in the houses that had been bombed and get people out. One Christmas he showed up, I was with my cousins and we were giggling all the time. There was a terrible row and he had turned over the table they were eating at, my mother and a few aunts and uncles. We weren't allowed in, I saw it and was rushed out. He was having a nervous breakdown. It left me with this feeling that any moment someone might go nuts and start shouting.

Every time I got married I thought someone might have a fit and stomp off. There would be a row. My Granny would row continuously, had a filthy temper. I got used to living within myself. I wasn't interested in sport, I just got along with it. I was sent to various schools for a day or two or a week in Devon, I learnt nothing. I remember 3am, one woman eating rice pudding from an enamel plate and she was shaking so much her fork or spoon went durrrrr – there was an excitement or thrill during the war.

Before the war comes to an end in 1944 I am sent back to Devon, and this is where, as far as I am concerned, my life starts. Devon at the point where we were at Torcross is near the point where all the ships and tanks were preparing for D-Day and it was full of Americans, sailors and all sorts, everything that you didn't know about you were confronted by. Food in vast quantities, they had P.K. rations that they were given every day that were waterproof, and you had five Pall Mall cigarettes in them, packet of dates, some chewing gum that you couldn't get in England then, health bar of some sort and a tin of granule coffee and Spam that nobody else liked but I rather liked it. There were huge tanks going around and machines that mended tanks and Devon is full of tiny roads and they would drive straight through everything. Every now and then a truck of American soldiers would drive through and they would say rude things and throw you P.K. rations. You met them occasionally walking around the village. I was nervous of country life, in that the village kids would torture animals like guillemots covered in oil that they would bury up to their necks in the sand and stone. I didn't like that and was considered a bit effete. They did anything like that. Any animal was crucified or tortured. There we were with all the soldiers and sailors practising landing on D-Day. Beesands village next to us, they were using live ammunition to practice, to keep them on their toes. One day they had a cock up and killed 600 of their own men. I didn't see it but it was only half a mile away. It was all hushed up. I learnt about it much later on, about 1948, this disaster. All the families were told their sons had died bravely in the war.

Moving on to VJ Day my mother is with a Canadian soldier who has got his arm round her in a complicated plaster on an arm crutch. She was keen to be with him without me. He told me to go away and I wouldn't, he gave me a shilling so I left.

When the war was over we came back to London and the place was flattened, not good, the people weren't the same, it wasn't jolly. Everyone was frightened stiff of V1 and V2s that would take out whole streets. The humour had gone. It really was depressed, sad and horrible. My father was doing even more work drawing children's comics as the paper rationing was over. I found myself living with a grandmother in Bloomsbury. My father's brother asked us to stay in his house in Brighton, it was only an hour on the train. That's where I met another crowd of interesting people. I met Canadian and American soldiers waiting to be shipped back. There were wonderful pubs down there and a collection of strange, odd people. I was 12 years old and I had a friend whose father owned a nightclub. Brighton was very racy and exciting, it was like Graham Greene's *Brighton Rock*, no police force worth a dime doing anything. Pubs open all hours, everyone was drunk as they were away from home. I got to know criminals, in those days they were Jewish criminals, they ran the joint. It was called The Burlesque Club. It was a racy drinking club with billiard tables upstairs and it had a 'blower' in it. A blower was a device that came directly from a race track and they paid rent for it and you had races beamed to the club, it was illegal but there you are. So all of these guys were putting money on horses and playing snooker. Occasionally going for each other with billiard cues, whacking each other. About three or four of them I thought they were the bees knees as they would take work on the big liners going in and out of New York, *Queen Elizabeth* or *Queen Mary*, and they would get jobs as barmen or waiters and get paid to go across and when they got back they bought things like clothes. American clothes were highly regarded, that you could not get here. There were no such things as jeans or trainers or any of the clobber that you see people in now. They were bringing it back and selling it at vast expense. Coloured socks, you couldn't get them in England anywhere. They would be second hand usually, pretty worn out, but you would swap them for something. I remember swapping a whole collection of German cigarette cards for an American tie that I now regret because the cards would be worth something now. The American tie had a phone dial on it and was very colourful. Then I got interested in all this clothing business and trying to get hold of jeans and mixing with all these people. Knowing the people in the club. There would be four or five people sitting at the bar, regulars, prostitutes, gays, sailors, killers, you name it they were all there. They paid me small amounts of money to get them sandwiches while they played snooker or cards. They would often play for 24 hours. I saw a guy who had a billiard cue through his chin that came

through his chin and out by his eye. Again it was an education to see these men, the way they talked, they had their own language, slang, I thought it was all pretty exciting and the town was exciting. Anyhow that was how I was brought up.

I was sent to a ridiculous school in Brighton. I still couldn't read and write by the age of 12, this was a church school again full of these funny priests trying to fiddle with you. So I had a high disregard for authority and the church that I never took seriously and don't now.

For reasons unknown to be me even today, even under the kosh, no one can bring it out of me.

I have no idea when I knew or why I should want to be a cartoonist. Certainly my father working as an illustrator of children's comics rather suggested it was a nightmare job and he hated it. As for humour I never saw a copy of *Punch* or anything like that. I didn't see the *Spectator*, which in those days wouldn't have had drawings in it, and as far as I know I never saw a copy of the *New Yorker* magazine. But I had picked up along the way the habit of going to the cinema on my own. And I'd go to news theatres. You'd go in for an hour and you would see a news reel, a cartoon, a trailer and a regular American comedy show, Joe MacDokes, Bar in the eight ball, American humour. I liked that, I thought it was pretty neat, all the fast talking, comedians, funny guys. I became rather enamoured with all things American. I am being influenced by outside, the schools I went to didn't seem to do anything for you.

Occasionally they would play music to you. We had a record player at home but didn't really play it much – a wind up 78, three minutes. I remember some poor teachers would teach music and I would hear people like Stravinsky and I thought that was terribly exciting, not knowing anything about it. I got rather interested in music. What with that with clothing, Americana, guys being amusing and Danny Kay, who was the bees knees, I thought that was the answer. Anyway not being able to read and write properly I could draw, a little bit. So I used to draw cartoons which I showed my mother. I kept on doing them until I was about 17 and I'm asked to go into the National Service. There was no war on and I didn't want to do it and I didn't want to do what my friends did to get out of it. That usually involved pretending to be mad or whatever and then being taken seriously and put away in some awful place like Haywards Heath. The other way was to flounce around and pretend to be gay and I knew about this and I had seen gay men and had a rough idea of what they did. They were after me but not madly. It didn't worry me. I knew about lesbians, sailors, men who liked to be tied up, all these louche people. I didn't want to harm myself getting out of the army, shooting my finger off or something. The house was full of old clothes. My father had a jacket, mackintosh, his clothes were all piled up. It was summer and I was sent to this man who was dentist, in those days they didn't have real psychiatrists, and I put all my fathers old clothes on thinking I was nuts or funny. They said what do you like

doing and I said, I'm very keen on Stravinsky, I like ballet and all the rest of it, I don't remember exactly. He listed me in grade 4, beyond help. I came out of that and I felt enormously guilty, there was no war but I felt strange and all the fears in my life came to one boiling point and I developed a very serious unhappiness and I couldn't talk to anyone about it. All my parents knew was that I was out of the army, national service and they didn't know why, it just said grade 4, instability or something like that and I didn't want to be doing nothing. In those days you didn't do nothing, it was considered a bit of a crime not to work or take any job. There was no afternoon television to plonk yourself in front of, there was this thing that you had to do something.

What happened next could have been due to my mother's friend, who had expensive cigarettes and everything, who put mother in touch with people, I don't know. Anyway I showed them my drawing and I went to *Punch* magazine and I'd already sent drawings to *Melody Maker* magazine and I had been introduced to jazz about the same time and I had got quite hooked on jazz pianist Thelonious Monk who was pretty obscure but I loved it. Again I was thinking about the *New Yorker*, I don't know why, I knew the names of some funny American writers, Robert Benchley, S. J. Perelman and Marx Brothers.

I didn't want to be at home as I hated it so I would leave every morning and get on a train to go to London, about seven shillings, with a portfolio, and go around Fleet Street. I was fearless in those days about selling myself as an illustrator, I wouldn't call myself a cartoonist at that time, and I got work immediately. I was being paid four pounds four shillings per drawing, or four guineas as it was in those days, up to seven pounds up to 25 pounds or whatever. I was earning quite good money. I also had this overwhelming feeling of loss and not knowing what I was doing. As I was never asked to do anything by my parents or had any discipline or aim. Instead of wandering the streets I became this cartoonist, and I was doing pretty well and I have been doing it ever since. Now I give it all away to various ex-wives but over the years I have done quite well out of it. I was with *Punch* for 35 years, until five years before it folded, more or less. Then I joined *Private Eye*, blah blah blah, I don't want to work for them anymore so I've left them. And now I do what I do, it's getting difficult in so much as most newspaper these days don't have cartoons anymore or anyone who can judge a gag or knows what a gag is. There is a certain creepy excitement about it at the moment, people are taking some interest. But they don't understand why someone would want to do it, why someone would want to do anything if you don't get 20 thousand pounds a day which is what they reckon you get being on tv or singing some dumb tune. They don't understand rejection or not being paid at all. Working for nothing. Thats it. Full stop.

BATTLE FOR BRITAIN DRAWINGS

"These shocking pictures have come to light of life before the mobile phone."

I have done thousands of cartoons and had lots of books published and they have all done very well but you don't make very much money out of them, but I've been paid for them already by *Private Eye* or *Punch* magazine. So they are being regurgitated. I have done some successful strips like *Great Bores Of The Day*, that ran for five years or maybe longer. Various other strips. I have never been a Gorr blimey cartoonist, I have always found it more fun observing the people around you, seeing how they look, how they dress, interesting clothing and all that. I am very interested in seeing how they react. People who think they're a hot number, they're it, forgetting that in five years there will be someone else who everyone is talking about. I am always interested in catching people out. One minute they are it, enjoying themselves, next minute they are hopeless. I always want to keep ahead of everyone. Watching how people talk and movies and tv and what young people get up to. I noticed lots of people who didn't want to read, just talk on the phone all the time, talking rubbish. I thought I would do a strip about that, about what you are not supposed to do. You are not supposed to talk about certain races, religions, genders, or do jokes about any of these things. Everyone is supposed to be equal, men are supposed to be the same as women, gender is talked about all the time. Remember I grew up at a time when men were supposed to be in charge but I noticed men were never in charge, women were always telling them what to do, how to eat and what they wanted. On the whole at that time most middle class men said yes dear, no dear and watched the cricket. So I decided to do a strip about all the electronic gimmicks like phoning that cut you off from people. They don't converse with you, just their friends, day and night. Once upon a time you might have lost your children to a teddy or pop singers, and now you are losing them entirely to mobiles. Several each, 24 hours a day, non stop. *Battle for Britain*. I did a previous one about the real battle of Britain. But this one is about young things now. I had this idea about using various school books, annuals from the 1930s onwards, before phones, like the Famous Five really. I like the way they were drawn, like my father drew, at great speed, and very little money. I get hold of these drawings and re-arrange them, or bits of them. I cut them up and alter them in some way, photocopy them and draw into them. So I keep the energy of the original drawing and have them talking to each other and running around. I change their hair to be like it is today, with mobiles and all running around in this world that once existed. Except there are phones everywhere, and I have changed the furniture. Without being snooty about them, because I didn't want to talk down to them in any way, I wanted to be respectful of them but to show them doing what they do. I have been running this strip for two years now. Now there is more and more interest in it.

I like to do cartoons that are not always instantly funny. I had an old cartoon friend when I worked for *Punch* who said to me that you must always do cartoons that they don't get. No-one else does it. I am not in the chain gang of cartoonists who are having to dream up cartoons of whatever is happening in politics or whatever and submitting them to a magazine or newspaper where upon the editor rejects them or not. The wastage for that is so horrible and you get no time to draw properly. I do political stuff as well. I have been doing the *Spectator* for 30 years now. I don't want to do political cartoons the way other people do them. They usually show a little man, saying worker, being hit over the head by another man saying city investor. Not that I am a fan or city investors or the city but that became a cliché. They tend to be left wing. I try to do them in a different way. I am still doing it.

I could go on all day. I used to work for left wing magazines, but left wing magazines don't want to pay. We are a dying breed (cartoonists), but it just requires the reader to have some knowledge of things. I don't want to sound snooty.

HEATH